creating
papercrafts

RYLAND
PETERS
& SMALL
LONDON NEW YORK

Labeena Ishaque

creating
papercrafts
stylish ideas and step-by-step projects

Senior designer Catherine Griffin

Senior editor Miriam Hyslop

Picture research Emily Westlake

Production Gemma Moules

Art director Anne-Marie Bulat

Publishing director Alison Starling

Stylist Labeena Ishaque

First published in the
United Kingdom in 2006 by
Ryland Peters & Small
20–21 Jockey's Fields
London WC1R 4BW
www.rylandpeters.com

10 9 8 7 6 5 4 3 2 1

Text, design and photographs
© Ryland Peters & Small 2006

ISBN-10: 1 84597 257 0

ISBN-13: 978 1 84597 257 8

A CIP record for this book is available
from the British Library.

Printed and bound in China

contents

introduction

Paper is a sensuous, versatile and fascinating material. It has been crafted by artisans and craftsmen for centuries and has infinite uses – from the practical to the decorative.

Paper takes its name from the word papyrus. Papyrus stems were used in Ancient Egypt as a basic material on which to write. Evidence of a similar ancient material, known as 'tapa', has also been found throughout the world.

The first recorded inventor of paper, as we know it today, is believed to be Ts'ai Lun in 105 AD. A Chinese courtier, Ts'ai Lun developed the art of papermaking whilst searching for a more practical alternative writing

LEFT Three-dimensional cardboard hearts have been pierced and threaded with ribbons and braids, then finished with tiny pearl beads to make adorable trinkets.

ABOVE Paper can be embedded with petals, leaves and grasses for a natural and tactile texture.

OPPOSITE CLOCKWISE FROM TOP LEFT A shop bought bag can be given a personal touch by removing the handle and replacing it with ribbon; Lorraine Dawkins's silk-screened images have been taken from old photos and taped to a white folded card; Tracing paper envelope inserts, maps and various papers make up the pages of this travel journal created by Darrell Gibbs. The envelopes are ideal for holding tickets, photos and postcards from your travels; Even the most basic white notelet can be transformed with a tiny stamped sunburst; Here glass votive holders have been wrapped in a metallic crêpe paper.

LEFT These pretty envelopes contain a colourful surprise – when opened, they reveal a richly-hued tissue lining. Perfect for invitations, they look great with matching cards.

RIGHT ABOVE Crêpe ribbon, flowers and leaves embellish this basic straw hat. The flowers can be changed to suit the colour of your outfit and dressed up or down with sequins and gems.

RIGHT CENTRE Old-fashioned paper-chains support these cheerful paper lanterns. They are child's play to make. Fold a rectangle of paper in half lengthways, cut away from the fold towards the edge, but not all the way down. Unfold, curve into a cylinder and glue the edges together.

RIGHT BELOW This cake has been decorated to give as a gift, with an array of various paper decorations. The wrapping consists of a blue and green tissue paper bands, gold paper leaves and a doily edging.

material to silk scrolls. He experimented with textile waste, including old fishing nets and rags. These were boiled and beaten, stirred into a pulp and spread onto a straining frame. When a thin tissue formed, the resultant paper was pressed beneath weights until dry.

Papermaking travelled to Japan with Buddhism. The Japanese embraced and refined the art of making paper and still create beautiful and long lasting papers today.

Over the next few centuries the art of papermaking travelled west, through Central Asia and Tibet, in to India and the Middle East, and finally arrived in Europe in the fourteenth century.

RIGHT Flower-embossed papers hang side by side with traditional Khadi paper, smooth, translucent sheets and heavier fibrous papers.

OPPOSITE ABOVE Swatches of Indian Khadi papers show the amazing scope for different textures and ingredients including grasses, petals and various natural fibres.

OPPOSITE CENTRE Rolls of cartridge and water colour papers illustrate how the edges of mould-made paper differ from handmade or machine-made papers. Handmade sheets tend to have fibres hanging free at the edges and machine-made papers are smooth edged and usually cut, whereas the mould-made sheets taper down and appear lighter at the edges than the rest of the sheet.

OPPOSITE BELOW A large pile of watercolour papers.

By the seventeenth century, Europe had a thriving papermaking industry. At first, paper was made mainly from cotton and linen rags. Rag paper was durable, absorbent and long lasting. With the huge demand for paper, technology soon stepped up to the mark.

Paper today is made using one of three methods of production. The first is the traditional handmade technique. Handmade paper is usually made sheet by sheet by pouring pulp into a mould (a frame with mesh stretched over it) and deckle (a frame that sits on top of the mould to shape the sheet of paper). The pulp is then carefully removed from the mould and deckle and left to dry. As the pulp dries and stiffens it becomes paper.

Mould-made paper is produced on a cylinder machine or a cylindrical mould revolving in a vat of paper pulp. Mould-made paper, which is very similar in appearance to

from wallpaper and packaging to newspapers and greeting cards, paper surrounds all aspects of our lives

handmade paper, has only two deckled (rough) edges, rather than four. Finally, machine-made paper is produced on a huge industrial scale. From advertising and publishing to tissues and train tickets, paper is big business.

With the widespread development of electronic media, paper has regained its rightful position as a creative material. Making beautifully crafted paper products has returned to being an art, rather than simply a mass produced commodity. From handmade greeting cards to gorgeous wrapped gifts, this book showcases dozens of ideas for crafting with paper – whatever your skills. Make the most of the beauty and versatility of paper and allow your creativity to flourish.

ABOVE Rolls of Washi, a traditional Japanese paper, are used to make many everyday objects in the Far East from Shoji screens to Bonbori lamps. 'Wa' translates as Japan and 'shi', paper.

MAIN PICTURE Handmade papers differ immensely in texture and weight. There is a huge difference between a heavy flax paper and a light and floaty Washi, for example.

OPPOSITE ABOVE Yesterday's newspaper can be thrown into the recycling bin, but it they are also the perfect material to reuse when making papier mâché. Its texture and density make it pourous and malleable enough to craft into all kinds of shapes and sizes.

OPPOSITE ABOVE LEFT Cupcake cases, with their delicate fluted edges, show how diverse a material paper is. A variety of papers are suitable for use in the kitchen including baking parchments and even edible rice paper.

OPPOSITE BELOW Bleached handmade flax paper has a wonderfully tactile quality.

cards and stationery

A handwritten note or a homemade greeting card are not only the oldest and most traditional means of correspondence but also the most personal. Take time to send a message to a friend – you never know, you might just make their day.

create your own stationery and send heartfelt
messages to your loved ones

ABOVE LEFT This is
a modern take on a
traditional decoupage
Valentine's Day card.
A hand-painted doily
frame surrounds
individually cut-out
letters, and a pretty
initialled heart charm
is fastened in place by
a decorative pin.

ABOVE RIGHT A trip to
the seaside and some
beachcombing can

uncover unusual
treasures, such as this
dainty heart-shaped
pebble. The corrugated
card backing has a thick
sharpness, which is an
excellent foil for the
smooth stone.

OPPOSITE ABOVE LEFT
We occasionally look at
old photographs that
have been hidden away in
family albums, but they're
often forgotten. Here,

family photos have been
given another lease of
life. Attached to plain
cards with photo-mount
corners, they make
attractive displays.

OPPOSITE ABOVE RIGHT
Here, a single leaf
skeleton is glued flat
onto a handmade card.
It's a striking example of
using an unassuming
object to its full
decorative potential.

OPPOSITE BELOW LEFT
A single element, such
as this feather, attached
to a papyrus background
creates a striking look
for an elegant thank-you
note or greeting card.

OPPOSITE BELOW RIGHT
Use ready-made mount
card to hold leftover
scraps of paper and a
selection of burnished
leaves collected from
your garden.

This pop-up card requires few materials and is simple to make. Take care when easing the sweeping staircase into shape as tearing the card could ruin the approach to your castle. Write your message on the back of the glitter card before attaching the decorative features.

PROJECT 1: pop-up greeting card

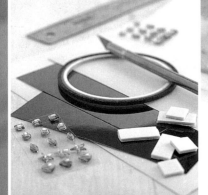

MATERIALS & EQUIPMENT
two pieces of glitter card: one measuring
22 x 30 cm (8½ x 12 in) for the backing,
one measuring 14 x 19 cm (5½ x 7½ in) for the castle
pink metallic card 13 x 13 cm (5 x 5 in) plus
two small squares for the windows
cutting mat • craft knife • ruler • pencil • double-
sided tape • sticky pads • self-adhesive jewels

1. Place the first piece of glitter card on the cutting mat with the shortest edge in front of you, score 7.5 cm (3 in) in from the top and bottom and fold in to the centre. Score a line 7.5 cm (3 in) in from the left hand edge and fold again. Open out the card and cut out the squares at the top and bottom left hand corners.

2. Use the castle template on p.104 and cut out. Draw around the template on the back of the second piece of glitter card (make sure you remember to draw the stairs). Using a sharp craft knife cut out the castle. Next, cut along the stairs, from left to right.

3. Push out the stairs, one by one, to create a sweeping staircase leading to the door of the castle. Take care not to tear the card. Fold along the bottom of the stairway to make a base. Next, take the pink metallic card and tape it to the centre of the backing glitter card.

4. Place sticky pads on the back of the castle and attach it to the centre of the card. Stick the base of the stairs to the bottom flap of the glitter card. Add small squares of metallic card for the windows, with double-sided tape and a few pink self adhesive jewels for a sparkling finishing touch.

festive stationery

Christmas wouldn't be Christmas without the deluge of cards posted to friends and family. Sending cards at Christmas is a relatively recent phenomenon, but it's now a multi-million-pound industry.

Handmade greeting cards were sent out on New Year's Eve in Germany from the 1400s. But the first known printed Christmas card dates back to 1843, sent by Sir Henry Cole, one of the founding directors of the South Kensington Museum, which was later to become the Victoria and Albert Museum. He commissioned artist John Calcott to design a card on his behalf, to send to his friends.

By the 1850s Christmas cards were commonplace and mass-produced. The first commercial Christmas card appeared in America in 1870, when a German immigrant, Louis Prang, sold printed cards from his lithographic shop in Massachusetts. These were very European in design, with flowers, leaves and trees, featuring nothing particularly religious, except for the words 'Merry Christmas' on each card, but they were the first seeds to be sown in the now gigantic Christmas cards industry.

LEFT This card is made using a simple paper-cutting technique, folded out to form a graphic, three-dimensional Christmas tree. To make the card, fold a thick piece of card in half. Open the card and draw half a tree shape inside the card, using the fold as the centre of the tree. Open out the card and, using a craft knife, carefully cut around the tree's outline. Finally, open out the tree to its full effect.

BELOW For a festive card that shimmers with style, cut a crown shape along the top of a folded card. Draw the rest of the crown on the front of the card and finish off with glitter and gold paints.

LEFT Tiny bundles of twigs are held together with metallic thread, sewn into place on a clean white card and finished off with name tags.

RIGHT Humble brown packaging paper is used here to make a cut-out Christmas tree.

BELOW LEFT Suspend a star in a window card. Attach fine thread to two points of the star, place it in the window and glue the thread onto the edge of the frame.

BELOW RIGHT Rubber stamps are quick and easy to use. Stamp with a steady hand to avoid any bleeding ink. Get stamps made to your own design or buy them with festive motifs.

The paper crafter's first outing is often with handmade Christmas cards. The luxurious quality of the metallic and pearlescent cards makes them perfect for crafting festive designs. The following projects involve simple cutting and embossing techniques, which are easy to grasp and yield stunning results.

PROJECT 2: Christmas cards

MATERIALS & EQUIPMENT
two pieces of pearlescent card and two pieces
of metallic card measuring 13 x 26 cm (5 x 10 in)
green card measuring 8 x 10 cm (3 x 4 in)
blue card measuring 9 x 11 cm (3½ x 4½ in)
ruler • pencil • cutting mat • craft knife
sticky pads • glue • embossing tool
snowflake stickers

1. Place the snowflake template (see p.104) at one end of the inside of a piece of metallic card, draw around it and cut out. Fold the metallic card in half. Cut a square of pearlescent card slightly larger than the snowflake motif and attach it to the inside front of the metallic card with sticky pads.

2. Take a piece of pearlescent card and fold in half. Using the sticky pads, attach the metallic snowflake from step 1 onto the front of the pearlescent card. Finish off both cards with novelty snowflake stickers.

1. Take the piece of green card and, using the angel or dove template on p.104, draw a festive motif on the back of the card. Next, take the embossing tool and press firmly around the outline of the motif (see techniques p.102).

2. Stick the green card to a piece of blue card with glue. Next, take a piece of metallic card and fold in half. Finally attach the blue card to the front of the backing card and finish with snowflake stickers.

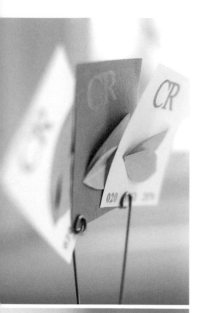

LEFT Standard business cards are ten a penny. Making your own cards will ensure that you stand out from the crowd. Here, gold lettering offsets the three-dimensional gold leaves that have been glued onto the card.

CENTRE LEFT AND RIGHT Use notepaper in toning colours instead of plain white. It's easy to make your own envelopes from handmade papers. Unfold a regular envelope to use as a pattern for your own.

BELOW LEFT Swatches of ticking fabric, cut with pinking shears, make ideal business cards for a textile designer. Print a card with personal details, tuck the fabric into a fold at the top and staple into place.

writing paper and envelopes

There is something special about receiving a handwritten letter in the post. Whether it's a note to say thank you or a friend just keeping in touch, when you hear the letterbox snap and see your name written neatly across an envelope, your spirits soar.

Most stationers sell a huge assortment of writing paper and envelopes in a wide range of colours, textures and finishes. From decorative handmade paper to colourful machine-made notepaper, there are a multitude of options to choose from.

Traditional watermarked weighty papers, reminiscent of times gone by, are incredibly durable and have a timeless quality. The fibres in handmade papers lie in random directions, making it much more resilient than machine-made paper. Papers made using a mechanized process, during which the fibres tend to be laid out in one direction, don't bond as well as their handmade counterparts, but they can be produced in bulk.

THIS PICTURE Create feminine floral headed paper by gluing dried, pressed flowers onto the notepaper. Go for a soft look with lavender and pink papers, trimmed with edging scissors and hole punches for a decorative border. Or, for a sharp contrast, attach a tiny sprig of flowers onto a sheet of graph paper.

INSET Make your own headed notepaper. Use gold inks and a fine paintbrush to create small patterns and shapes at the top of the page. Gold works well with crisp white papers as well as on darker and stronger colours (especially blues and purples for a regal look).

Creating your own stationery could not be simpler. When dealing with your personal correspondence surround yourself with beautiful writing paraphernalia: ink fountain pens, stacks of gorgeous papers; even wax seals for an extra special finishing touch to a sealed envelope. Add personality to notepaper and envelopes with little details, such as cutting out decorative borders or gluing dried pressed flowers to edges. Make your own letterheads by embossing your initials to the top of the page, or even have your own stamps made. From personalized business cards to birthday or Christmas cards, pop-up to decoupage, rediscover the delights of crafting stationery that is both stylish and unique.

ABOVE LEFT The wax-sealed scroll was once the means of securing a note. Go back in time and write invites on Khadi paper, roll into a scroll and seal them with your own stamp. But remember: this is only suitable for hand delivery.

ABOVE RIGHT This business card, printed on recycled brown card, features a delicate skeleton leaf sprayed gold and glued to the centre – a perfect design for a tree surgeon, landscape gardener or arborist.

OPPOSITE LEFT Pressed leaves age and quickly crumble and fade. To ensure that their beautiful colours and textures live on, colour-photocopy pretty leaves onto handmade paper and card.

OPPOSITE RIGHT Old receipts, vouchers and tickets make unusual and original cards. Attach feathers, leaves and other natural finds, too. The key to a successful collage is to stick to similar colours and textures.

gift wrapping

The old adage 'It is better to give than to receive' rings true when preparing to wrap a gift. There is real pleasure to be had in concealing a carefully selected present in layers of crisp tissue, under a gorgeous wrapping; then tying the ribbon with a flourish; and watching it being carefully unwrapped by the recipient.

wrapping paper

There is such an enormous range of wrapping paper available these days that it can take almost as long to choose the paper as the gift itself. From humble brown packaging paper to the most luxurious flocked and hand-painted papers, the choice is endless.

To create a beautifully wrapped gift, use anything from simple, single coloured crêpe papers and dress them up with ribbons, or go wild with clashing papers, ribbons and a gift tag. Unify a group of presents by covering them in toning colours but with different textured papers. Unusual combinations – such as brown paper with velvet ribbons and sequins, or layers of Japanese lace papers over muted shades of tissue – make eye-catching and unique wrapped gifts.

Larger or awkward-shaped gifts can be a chore to wrap, but a little thought can go a long way. Create patchworks of different papers, or sew two large sheets of paper together at three sides, making a bag that can be tied closed with a ribbon or braid.

ABOVE The script paper looks neat bound with a strip of contrasting Khadi paper and raffia ties.

RIGHT Newspaper tied with twine makes an inexpensive and stylish gift wrapping.

OPPOSITE TOP, LEFT TO RIGHT Unify a group of gifts by matching or toning colours; A metallic chocolate-brown paper tied with a thin velvet ribbon gives this gift a slick, masculine feel; Finish off a wrapped gift with a raffia tie – separate the strands at the knot to create a bow effect.

OPPOSITE CENTRE, LEFT TO RIGHT This wonderful snakeskin-print paper needs little embellishment, but the beige linen ribbon gives it a sophisticated finish; Add detail to a solid coloured paper by gluing on fabric leaves and tying with a sheer ribbon; A crisply printed Art Deco paper is given the ultimate in luxurious embellishment with thick velvet ribbons and diamanté buckles.

OPPOSITE BELOW, LEFT TO RIGHT This camouflage-wrapped gift is given a lift by the deep orange paper twine with knotted ends; This gift has a really Eastern feel to it, with its fabric-like ruched paper and double ribbon ties; The flower- and leaf-embedded papers, alongside the pulpy textured paper, create a nature-inspired look.

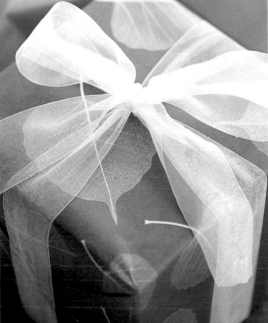

This method of wrapping gifts is great for bottles, jars and vases. More awkward shapes can be rolled in a sheet of thin card to create a cylinder, before being wrapped.

PROJECT 3: wrapping solution

MATERIALS & EQUIPMENT
gift wrapping paper
double-sided tape or glue
tissue paper in two colours
(pink and green shown)
ruler • scissors

1. Measure the length and diameter of the cylinder. Cut the gift wrapping paper to fit the cylinder, allowing a 1 or 2 cm (½ or ¾ in) overlap at each end. Roll the paper around the cylinder (leaving enough to cover both ends equally). Secure the paper along the length with double-sided tape or glue.

2. Starting at one end of the cylinder, begin to pleat the paper in towards the centre, keeping it as tight and neat as possible. Overlap each pleat until you reach the end. Secure the last pleat firmly with double-sided tape. Repeat at the opposite end.

3. Take the pink tissue paper and fold it in three lengthways, about 10 cm wide (4 in) and long enough for the ends to meet when wrapped around the cylinder. Cut a sheet of green tissue paper in half and fold 1-cm-wide (½-in) concertina pleats lengthways.

4. Wrap the pink tissue paper around the cylinder and secure with tape or glue. Tie the concertinaed green tissue band in a knot around the pink tissue. Cut either end at a slant, to create a zigzagged edge, and pull out into a fan shape.

THIS PICTURE Wrap a bottle of wine in brightly-coloured tissue paper and secure using a sticky label. This can be inscribed with a patterned border and personalized for the recipient.

OPPOSITE TOP TO BOTTOM Take two pieces of card in contrasting colours and cut one rectangle smaller than the other. Cut a basic leaf shape out of the smaller one, then glue it onto the larger card for a strong silhouette image; Cut a star shape out of a gift tag and cover the window with gold tissue paper; Another simple way to decorate a tag is to cut shapes from a contrasting paper and glue them into place; Add extra details by attaching stars and tying to the tag through a punched hole.

ABOVE LEFT Colour-photocopy a map to use as wrapping. If you have any remnants left, glue a piece onto a white gift tag.

ABOVE RIGHT A handmade gift tag comprising, very basically, a small rectangle of cartridge paper with handwritten name and painted leaf.

BELOW Use a craft knife and cutting mat to cut out a relief shape on a dark card with a white interior.

gift tags

If you are taking care to wrap a gift beautifully, the cherry on the cake has to be a tag. You could buy tags to match the gift wrap, but how about creating your own? Gift tags are so easy to make. To coordinate your tag with your chosen gift wrap, use remnants of the wrapping paper and simply glue them onto the tag. Alternatively, take a motif or colour from the wrapping paper design and use an original papercrafting technique, such as embossing or cutting, to enhance and complement it.

Be inventive. Luggage labels and old greetings cards can be recycled; plain cards embellished with sequins, leaves, feathers and stickers. The simplest scrap of card can be painted, stamped, collaged and cut and transformed from ordinary to eye-catching. Create gift tags that hint at what is underneath the gift wrapping – a glittery champagne-flute-shaped tag for a bottle of bubbly; heart-shaped tags tied with lace for a romantic gift. Use your imagination and go with it.

gift bags and boxes

One of the thrills of receiving a gift from a designer shop is often the luxurious packaging. Who can resist the lure of the instantly recognizable powder-blue Tiffany & Co box, the deep orange of the Hermès packaging or the saucy pink and black glossy carrier bag from Agent Provocateur? Whether the gift is a simple silver keyring, a beautiful leather purse or the sexiest lingerie you can imagine, the gift box is an inherent part of the deal. Use this kind of packaging as a source of inspiration. Every time you receive a gift you love, make a note of how it is wrapped and remember it when you wrap your gifts for friends.

So many things that you buy these days come in boxes. Instead of throwing empty boxes in a recycling bin, keep hold of a few and customize them. For a truly professional look, they can be painted, decoupaged, embellished, lined with layers of tissue paper and finished off with luscious ribbons. Likewise, paper carrier bags can be transformed. Exchange the handles for ribbons and braids, glue decorative paper patches on, or attach beads and buttons, labels and tags.

ABOVE LEFT Decorate a shop-bought box by gluing sequins randomly all over the base and lid. Finish with beads attached to a thick gold wire.

ABOVE RIGHT Individually boxed confectionery is perfect for a party favour. Place a petit four or truffle in a tiny box lined with a cute little paper case.

BELOW Breathe new life into a plain white paper bag with a luxurious grosgrain ribbon and a gorgeous diamanté buckle. Cut two slits at the base of each handle, thread the buckle onto the ribbon and thread the ribbon in through the slots. Secure the ribbon inside the bag with glue.

ABOVE RIGHT These plain white boxes with scalloped edges have been folded tightly together and tied closed with layers of beautiful jewel-bright Indian ribbons.

LEFT Holes have been punched and rivets added to the top of a textured paper pouch, which has an unusual velvety embossed pattern. Rivet kits can be bought from most haberdashery stores.

ABOVE LEFT Use metallic tissue paper to fold together mini bags. To make them, take apart a paper bag, photocopy the outline (reduce its size) and use it as a template. Tie closed with a sheer ribbon and a beaded fruit decoration.

FAR LEFT Attach a pocket to the front of a gift bag to hold cards or gift vouchers. Tie the handles closed with rick-rack braiding and tassels.

These little boxes are perfect for giving confectionery. They are ideal to make as favour boxes to give at weddings or parties. Reduce or increase the template to suit your purposes.

PROJECT 4: bonbon boxes

MATERIALS & EQUIPMENT
white card • decorative paper • ribbon
adhesive spray • pencil • cutting mat
scissors • craft knife • hole punch
metal ruler • double-sided tape

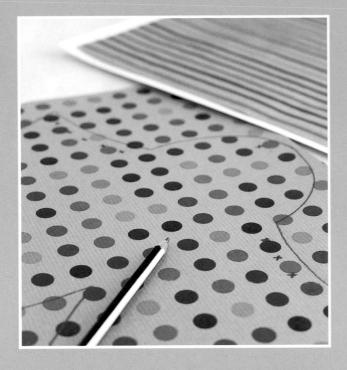

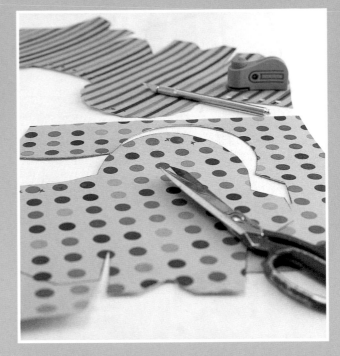

1. Stick the decorative paper onto the white card using the adhesive spray, taking care to cover the entire sheet with spray mount. Use the box template on p.105 and draw around it on the patterned card, marking off the tabs.

2. Cut out the box shape, using scissors for the main body and a craft knife at the more intricate parts. Take the hole punch and punch a row along two of the curved edges and one hole at the top centre of each flap.

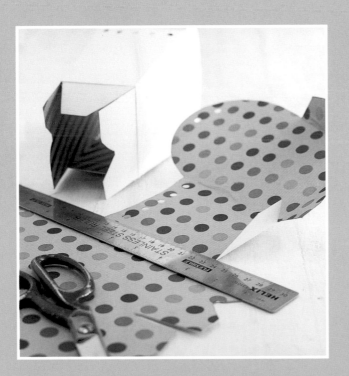

3. Fold along the dotted lines, using a metal ruler as a guide. Press along the fold with the handles of a pair of scissors to create a neat, sharp crease. Fold the sides of the box in towards each other and secure them with double-sided tape at the flaps.

4. Tuck the bottom flaps together and secure with double-sided tape. Thread the length of ribbon through the holes on the top flaps. Gently curve the opening flaps together and neatly tie together with the ribbon.

LEFT A simply wrapped square box is embellished with a tiny bouquet of paper flowers, secured with sheer and gingham ribbons. Paper flowers can be found in most haberdashery stores.

BELOW LEFT The faint daisy-print pattern on this gift wrap is mirrored by the floral braid looped around the corners of the box. The theme is followed through with a single flower glued onto the tag.

BELOW RIGHT Get inventive with old shirt buttons and thread them onto thick silk for a stylish finish.

OPPOSITE MAIN PICTURE A strip of decorative tissue paper has been pleated and punched and finished with a zigzagged border. A fine jeweller's wire has been threaded through the paper to secure it around the gift, so creating a soft, Japanese look.

OPPOSITE TOP LEFT A stroll along the beach often ends with a pocket full of shells. Thread them onto paper twine and drape over textured paper.

OPPOSITE TOP CENTRE A sequinned three-dimensional star adds a glittery touch to this muted metallic box, while the matt silver paper is a perfect foil for the shimmer of the sequins.

OPPOSITE TOP RIGHT Holes punched randomly through a brown paper strip add further texture to this package, which has been wrapped in mould-made pulp paper. The strip has been cut using pinking shears for a scalloped edge and threaded through with twine.

embellishments

Embellishing a simply wrapped gift can transform it from an unassuming present into something quite special. A little thought can go a long way. Hint at what's under the paper. For example, when wrapping a set of chopsticks or rice bowls, cover them in a Chinese newspaper and finish with silver leaf and a jade ribbon. If you are wrapping a sweater use tissue paper and then tie with thick yarn, instead of ribbon, and make mini knitting needles out of wooden cocktail sticks to add a bit of fun and intrigue.

A plain brown packaging paper can be given a lift with a sumptuous ribbon or a thin strip of richly decorated paper. Tiny paper flower bouquets or pretty nature finds can be attached to wrapped gifts as a stylish finishing touch. Keep a crafty box of tricks to hand. Collect trimmings, beads, buttons and braids when you see them. Carefully unwrap gifts that you have received and keep the ribbons and scraps of paper. The winter sales at department stores and haberdashery shops are a good time to stock up on such items.

home decoration

A home is a great place to display and use paper. As its decorative and durable qualities are being rediscovered, there is an influx of designer paper products on the market – from lighting, screens and furniture to rugs and soft furnishings.

paper at home

Paper has long been used in the home as a practical and decorative medium: from the traditional Japanese 'shoji' screens to the hand-painted wallpapers of the fifteenth-century French courts; and from the papier mâché furniture found in fashionable Victorian homes, right through to the recycled cardboard chairs and tables widely available today.

Today, interior designers and artisans recognize paper's versatility, charm and strength, and more and more are using it to make chic decorations for the home. From lampshades and picture frames to vases and bowls, paper products bring something special to an interior.

Because paper is such an inexpensive material, it is ideal for making seasonal changes throughout the house. Consider how elements are put together in your home and use the final touches and accessories to tie a look together. Introduce a cosy autumnal feel with golden lanterns adorning shelves and matelpieces, or substitute a soft pink paper blind for one in chocolate brown, to instantly refresh your surroundings.

ABOVE LEFT Divide living spaces or adorn windows with paper flowers. Here, red and yellow tissue paper flowers, which are often seen at Indian weddings, have been threaded onto a wooden stake to make a stylish screen.

ABOVE RIGHT A great alternative to the net curtain is to attach translucent Japanese Washi to a window. Use spray mount to stick it to the window frame. Decorate the paper with small flowers cut from a thick Khadi paper.

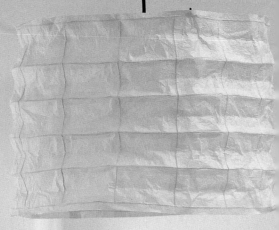

ABOVE LEFT Display unusual paper details in your home. The beautiful rose-printed packaging of these incense sticks adds a hint of the Orient to your interior.

ABOVE RIGHT The traditional Japanese paper light is given a modern twist with its strong deep-red Thai paper stretched over a tall wire frame.

ABOVE RIGHT This crumpled paper lampshade is based on the traditional Japanese Bonbori. The translucent paper softens the artificial light to a warm glow in this bright white room.

THIS PICTURE AND BELOW RIGHT There are many papers that look and feel like fabric, such as and these pillowcases. The paper has been embroidered with silk thread and lined with linen fabric.

CLOCKWISE FROM TOP LEFT These fairy lights have been boxed individually with paper cubes and give a soft, diffused glow; The interesting details here are the tiny V-shapes cut into the paper shade, which are folded back to reveal triangles of light showing through the shade; Each light is shrouded in a miniature paper flower, giving the impression of illuminated blooms.

BELOW A string of fairy lights with papier mâché shades creates an unusual and eye-catching feature hung along a mantelpiece. The frames for the shades have been structured with wire. Tibetan handmade paper has been by soaked in a diluted wallpaper paste and draped across the frames in layers, then sealed with PVA glue to achieve a soft sheen.

lampshades

Lighting is a vital part of any home. Used successfully, it can enhance a room and heighten atmosphere. Strip lights and large overhead lights are perfect for work areas, but too harsh for living and sleeping spaces, where intimacy and relaxation are crucial.

Paper is an ideal material for diffusing light as it can be produced in so many different weights and textures. It has been used for lanterns and lampshades in the Far East for centuries, from the simple white paper ball popular in Japan to the brightly coloured festive lanterns used in Chinese New Year celebrations.

As a working material, paper is easy to handle — it can be woven, bonded, cut and then slotted back together, and papier-mâchéd over a wire frame. All these qualities have made paper a popular choice for lighting since ancient times, and will probably be used for centuries to come.

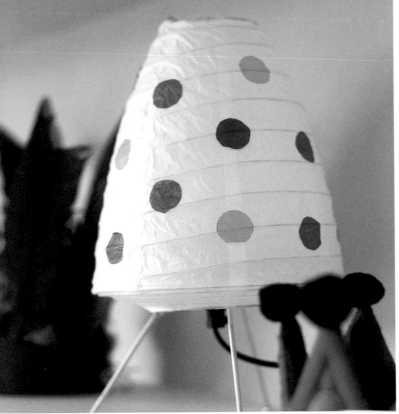

LEFT A small paper bedside lamp is customized with cheerful polka dots. To recreate this look, cut circles out of brightly coloured tissue paper and use glue or spray mount to stick them onto the shade in a random pattern.

BELOW Here, tiny fairy lights are covered by colourful miniature paper drum shades. The lights highlight the antique toy collection on the shelf above and create a magical mood that looks great in a child's bedroom or nursery.

It can be difficult to find the right lampshade to suit your interior. Here is the ideal solution: a plain white cylindrical shade transformed with tissue paper. Use a single statement colour or a combination such as eau de nil, powder blue and deep red. Try experimenting with thicker strips of paper or with folds and pleats for a textured effect.

PROJECT 5: striped lampshade

MATERIALS & EQUIPMENT
plain white cylindrical lampshade
tissue paper (cream, white, pale
blue, eau de nil and crimson) or
a selection of paper ribbons
scissors • craft knife
PVA glue

1. Cut strips of tissue paper approximately 5 mm–1 cm (¼–½ in) wide and the length of the lampshade (allowing extra to overlap at each end). Apply a thin line of glue along the top and lower edges of the shade.

2. Take the first strip of tissue paper and stick inside the top of the frame, overlapping slightly. Carefully stretch the strip as tight as it will go and tuck it in at the lower edge. Press firmly.

3. Repeat step 2 until the entire lampshade is covered with coloured paper. Stick the strips as closely together as possible selecting the colours at random.

4. To finish off, trim the excess tissue at the top and bottom of the frame with the craft knife. Apply a thin layer of glue along the edges to secure and set the tissue paper in place.

LEFT Create a botanical display by gluing pressed foliage onto antique or aged cards, which can be picked up in flea markets and charity shops. Alternatively, you can age paper and card by wiping a damp teabag over its surface and allowing to dry.

BELOW A wood-block-printed initial adorned with a decorative pin is a touching addition to a box frame of mementos.

BELOW RIGHT Gather a selection of images that will work well together. Then display them in handmade frames of different sizes but made from the same material.

THIS PICTURE Heavily embossed paper is an ideal material for picture frames. The great thing about making your own frames is that you can tailor-make them to fit your choice of image, whether it is a much-loved photograph, old postcard or a even a beautiful picture cut from the pages of a magazine.

FAR RIGHT AND INSET Corrugated cardboard is a robust material that can withstand any number of knocks and falls. Here, a full-length hinged screen is made from layers cardboard bonded together.

picture perfect

From an unassuming, neutral background to a flamboyantly luxurious and decorative feature, paper can be crafted to create the perfect frames for your photography, postcards or artwork. Make simple sleeves for pictures by folding a piece of card and cutting out a window at the front. For the most basic of frames, place the photo inside the card, facing out, and then seal.

Go all out and fashion frames from moulded papier mâché or layers of corrugated card, to create a substantial and sturdy frame. Shop-bought frames, such as the inexpensive clip ones available from all stationers, can be given a lift by mounting an image onto a background of textured or decorative paper and then sealing it inside the glass frame. One can even mount little objects onto heavier cards, such as dried leaves, beads and buttons glued onto a background, and hang on the wall with ribbons.

This simple yet effective picture frame can be created using any combination of colours. Choose strong, bright colours to offset a black-and-white photograph or soft pastels to compliment a favourite print.

PROJECT 6: rainbow picture frame

MATERIALS & EQUIPMENT
six pieces of foam board, five measuring
25 x 21 cm (10 x 8½ in), one measuring
5 x 20 cm (2 x 8 in) for the stand
five sheets of gift wrap measuring 29 x 25 cm
(11½ x 10 in) • ruler • craft knife • cutting mat
clear tape • masking tape • pencil

1. For the frame, take one of the six pieces of foam board and cut a window measuring 14 x 10 cm (5½ x 4 in), which will leave a 5.5 cm (2 in) border. Next, place the foam board on the back of a sheet of metallic paper.

2. Fold all four corners of the metallic paper, followed by the sides, on to the back of the frame and attach with clear tape. Next, tape small strips of metallic paper into each corner of the window. Take a craft knife and score an X from opposite corner to opposite corner (see above).

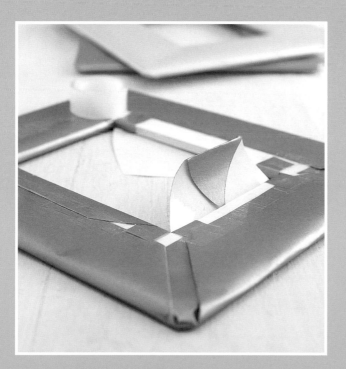

3. Fold back the flaps and attach to the back of the frame. Repeat steps 1 and 2 with three more pieces of board. Sandwich the four frame pieces together with double-sided tape. For the back, cover the remaining large piece of foam board with paper and tape to the rest of the frame, leaving the top open.

4. For the stand, cover the smaller piece of foam board with metallic paper. Next, score along its width 3 cm (1¼ in) down and fold along the score. Tape to the back of the frame at the short folded end, 3 cm (1¼ in) down from the centre.

ABOVE This basket has been made from twisted lengths of newspaper that have been woven together to form a rattan-like finish – great for storage, but perhaps not the most practical bag to carry in the rain.

LEFT These papier mâché pulp bowls are made by Maggie Hollingworth. Using pull-out sections from a newspaper, such as the pink financial pages, gives the pulp different colours and softer hues.

decorative details

When adding the finishing touches to your home decor, think how the colours, textures and surfaces combine to create the overall look. Whether folded, pleated, woven, hole-punched, layered or even pin-pricked, paper details can all contribute to the finished look of your decorating scheme.

A neutral-toned space, with white or muted furniture and walls, is a good foil for brightly coloured paper accessories. This is a simple and inexpensive way to add depth and detail to a room, without having to change the larger features within the room. If a room is colourful to begin with, detailing can be introduced with textural papers. A Japanese Washi paper can be folded and pleated to give more dimension to a lampshade, and corrugated cardboard can be glued together in layers to create a wonderfully abstract texture as a screen.

LEFT AND RIGHT
Galvanized metal
flower pots have been
customized with Chinese
festive papers, then
glued into place and
secured with twine.
PVA is the ideal glue
to use, as it allows for
some movement and
dries clear. It is an
alternative take on
decoupage, but instead
of the old-fashioned
Victorian images bold
graphic images are used
for a modern and more
dramatic look.

LEFT Judy Simmons'
beautiful papier mâché
bowls are made by
layering strips of paper
over a mixing bowl.
Once the basic shape
has been prepared, it
is removed from the
mould and layered over
with torn tissue and
decorative paper.

RIGHT Libby Lister's
crêpe paper flower is
given a realistic touch
with tinted petals. Use
a fine felt-tipped pen or
water-colour to paint it.

Papier mâché is a great technique for creating bowls and platters. Once set, papier mâché can be painted, varnished, découpaged, embellished or covered in delicate Asarakushi paper.

PROJECT 7: papier mâché bowl

MATERIALS & EQUIPMENT
newspaper • pink Japanese Asarakushi paper
bowl (as a mould) • clingfilm
wallpaper paste • paint brushes
dark brown acrylic paint

1. Wrap the exterior of the bowl in clingfilm. Tear the newspaper into strips, making larger strips for the main body of the bowl and smaller strips for the curved edges. Prepare the wallpaper paste. Take a strip of newspaper, cover both sides with the paste and place on top of the clingfilm.

2. Continue to layer the strips of newspaper over each other, criss-crossing them as you go. You will probably need about six layers. Leave to dry for at least 24 hours. Once the paper is dry, gently unwrap the clingfilm and remove the papier mâché casing from the mould.

3. Paint the bowl with a couple of layers of acrylic paint. Allow the first coat of paint to dry before starting the next. When the paint is dry, tear two lengths of Japanese Asarakushi paper slightly larger than the bowl.

4. Brush a thin layer of wallpaper paste over the inside of the bowl and carefully place one of the sheets of Asarakushi paper into the bowl. Repeat with the outside of the bowl. Trim away the excess strands of paper and let dry.

keepsakes

Mementos of days gone by come in all shapes and sizes – love notes, Polaroids snapped on exotic holidays, mud-splattered tickets from music festivals. These precious little nothings can disappear over time. By making your own keepsakes, however, you can gather them together and enjoy a nostalgic trip down memory lane.

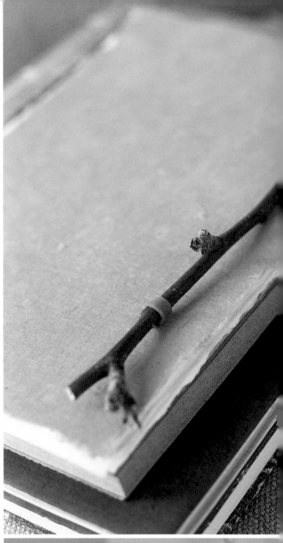

LEFT This shop-bought address book has a homemade floral cover with sprigs of spring lilac adorning the jacket. Cover books with remnants of wallpaper, gift wrap or handmade paper embossed with petals for a similar look.

RIGHT Make a notebook from a block of watercolour paper, covered with torn Khadi paper sheets. Tear the covers to size, and place into position. Hold the pages together by punching holes at the top and bottom edges of the left-hand side, thread an elastic band through the holes and secure with a twig.

journals, albums and scrapbooks

There is something to be said about the practicality of a Personal Digital Assistant system, where all the information and notes you might need can be stored in one tiny space – your address book, diary, sketchbook, notebook, journal, even a phone or camera, all rolled into one. However, in these times of the sleek metal keypad, there is still a demand for tactile, beautiful and inspiring books and journals.

You might want to buy books off the shelf that can be customized to suit your purpose or style. Create travel journals by slotting envelopes, maps and tracing-paper inserts into a book and attach photos and tickets from your travels. Or why not make files for your favourite recipes with laminated pages to wipe clean, or a scrapbook for keeping natural treasures found on country walks? Cut newspaper clippings from important days and put them beside photographs in your own special photo album. For a baby memory box, use wallpaper from the nursery to cover a homemade box and collect everything from baby's hospital wrist tag to cards and a lock of hair. Be inventive and creative with the way you store and display your keepsakes.

THIS PICTURE Darrell Gibbs makes beautiful notebooks and stationery from recycled papers. Here, he has bound together envelopes and photocopies of old documents to create this inspired journal.

FAR LEFT This sketchbook has been given a handle, for portability. Simply punch two holes down the left-hand side of the pages, add a loose binding with a strip of brown paper and thread through a simple garden twine.

LEFT The edges of these notebooks have been stitched through with linen thread. These stitches hold the pages securely inside the textured paper covers and are also a striking decorative feature.

ABOVE TOP LEFT A lovely way to present individual photos is to mount them in tissue-lined double-folded cards, tied with sheer ribbons. They can also be used as frames – simply fold back the covers and stand up.

ABOVE LEFT A collection of delicate shell buttons is displayed in a paper box frame. Take two identical pieces of sturdy paper and measure a 4-cm (1½-in) border around the entire edge of each sheet, score with a sharp craft knife and fold up. Sew the buttons into the centre of one sheet, with the folded edges facing up and cut a square out of the centre of the other. Place the frame, folded edges face down over the buttons, and secure folded edges together with glue.

ABOVE Larger photos, sketches and paintings can be kept in an old-fashioned portfolio case. This one is made with two large pieces of card, secured together down one side with linen-backed tape. The corners have been covered with the same tape and the opening is tied together with a linen ribbon.

OPPOSITE BELOW Photocopy and enlarge a holiday photo to cover a photo album. This image had been copied onto a heavy watercolour paper and the pages have been bound together with a glossy grosgrain ribbon.

ABOVE, CLOCKWISE FROM TOP LEFT These albums are made from recycled card. The thinner albums are bound and stitched by machine, using a large zigzag stitch. Thicker albums probably won't go through a sewing machine, so punch holes and hand-sew the edge; Use a translucent and fibrous Japanese paper to make a large envelope. Fold in three corners of a square of paper, corner to corner, and glue together. Sew a button or toggle onto the remaining corner and loop over a length of cotton thread to fasten the envelope; Score slits into pages of a journal or album and use paper clips, slipped into the slits, to hold cards and pictures in place.

This scrapbook has been devised to hold all the bits and pieces that you might accumulate on your travels – from tickets and maps to photos and postcards. Use as many different types of paper as you like and don't forget, you can always add more travel souvenirs later.

PROJECT 8: travelogue

MATERIALS & EQUIPMENT
A4 (8½ x 11 in) cartridge paper, graph paper and tracing paper • world map
leatherette paper • hole punch • twine • needle
ruler • glue or adhesive spray

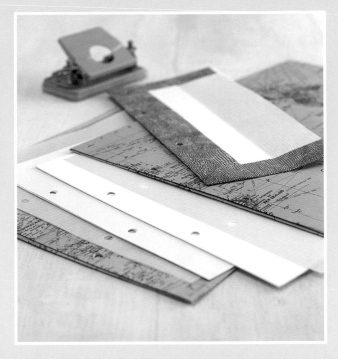

1. To make the cover, take two sheets of cartridge paper and cover them with a map of the world using adhesive spray. Next, organize a pile of cartridge paper, graph paper and tracing paper. Using the hole punch, punch two holes down the left hand side of each sheet of paper and the front and back covers.

2. Cut out a piece of cartridge paper, measuring 23 x 8 cm (11 x 3 in), then cover with the leatherette paper. Fold the leatherette-covered paper in half, lengthways, and punch holes along the two long edges with the holes in the other sheet of paper.

3. Starting with the back cover, assemble all of the pages (lining up the holes) and finish with the front cover. For the binding, fold the leatherette-covered paper along the left-hand side of the travelogue. Take the twine and sew together (see above). Secure with a knot.

4. For the finishing touches, cover each corner of the map with a small triangular piece of leatherette paper using glue. Finally, attach a short length of twine to the back inside cover and a small disc of map-covered cartridge paper to the front cover using a needle and cotton. Tie the twine around the disc to secure.

ABOVE LEFT Magazine file boxes can be livened up by covering them with attractive papers. These elegant boxes are covered in photocopies of old handwritten French documents.

ABOVE RIGHT Store crafty bits and bobs in individual boxes and label them by gluing a sample of its contents onto the front of the lid. These boxes contain buttons, shells, fabric and feathers.

BELOW LEFT Stationery shops sell containers for storing specific office items, like this linen-bound CD storage box. The simple, typed index card details the boxes' contents.

BELOW RIGHT Decoupage and line a special memento box with torn scraps of paper from an old book found in a charity shop or flea market.

RIGHT AND CENTRE RIGHT Utilitarian brown cardboard boxes are stacked up in the bedroom. These boxes hold shoes and, to save opening the boxes to find the right shoe, each is labelled with a Polaroid of the pair that is stored within.

BELOW RIGHT To organize your home office, label archive boxes with self-adhesive labels. Stack them in groups for an attractive display.

storage solutions

A great way to store all kinds of trinkets and keepsakes is to box them up and place them neatly on open shelving. Not only is this a practical storage solution but you could also group the boxes together to make an attractive display.

Sturdy flat-packed boxes can be bought from larger department and out-of-town furniture stores. These can be kept plain and utilitarian, simply marked with self-adhesive labels and stacked one on top of the other. Or create handles for them so they can be pulled out of a pile with ease: cut two slots down the sides of a box, thread through rope, cord or ribbon, then knot on the inside.

Use shoeboxes to store not only shoes, but also old documents, crafting items, trinkets and ribbons. Label them up by attaching whatever is in the box onto the lid. With larger flat boxes, like chocolate boxes, make card grids to slot inside and keep trinkets and mementos organized – this kind of box is particularly good for costume jewellery and beads. Boxes are the ideal organizational tool, especially for collectors or hoarders, but as you can see they can also be beautiful decorative items.

A keepsake box is an ideal gift for new parents. Great for collecting cards, first bootees and even hospital wrist tags, a memory box is the perfect place to store all the precious things that come with a baby. This design could be modified for weddings and other special occasions, too.

PROJECT 9: baby memory box

MATERIALS & EQUIPMENT
2 pieces of thick white card: one measuring 28 x 33 cm (11 x 13 in) for the box,
one measuring 25 x 46 cm (10 x 18 in) for the lid • stapler • ruler • pencil
craft knife • cutting mat • glue • scissors • pinking shears • embroidered paper
cartridge paper (cream and blue) • ribbons • self-adhesive velcro
large safety pin • photograph

1. For the box, mark 18 x 23 cm (7 x 9 in) 5 cm (2 in) in from the edge of the card. Cut a triangle into each corner of the card (see above). Next, score along the interior rectangle with a craft knife and fold away to form the base. Staple the triangular flaps inside the box. For the lid, measure in 20 cm (8 in) from each end of the card and score a 6-cm (2-in) wide spine.

2. Cover and line the box and lid with the embroidered paper, folding in all the raw edges for a neat finish. Next, place the box on the inside of the lid, lining the side of the box up with the inside of the spine (so the cover closes over the box like a book). Glue the box to the inside of the lid.

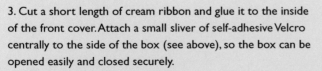

3. Cut a short length of cream ribbon and glue it to the inside of the front cover. Attach a small sliver of self-adhesive Velcro centrally to the side of the box (see above), so the box can be opened easily and closed securely.

4. To finish the box, glue the blue ribbon around the lower edge of the cover and attach a large safety pin to the ribbon. Cut a small piece of cartridge paper with pinking shears, for a decorative edge, and glue the baby's photograph to it, tuck it into the ribbon.

table settings

With a little time and imagination, you can create table settings and accessories that are both stylish and original. Making your own decorative touches for a meal with friends will not only heighten your sense of anticipation but also delight your guests.

festive tables

Christmas is the one time of the year when most of us decide to get the napkins and candles out for a celebratory meal at home. With the profusion of festive decorations on sale it's easy to be seduced by the excesses of fairy lights and glitter. However, it can be much more satisfying and enjoyable to use your papercrafting skills to put together a table setting of your own.

Use anything from brown packaging paper to doilies and tissue paper. The most basic materials can be worked into a theme and you can be as inventive and experimental with your ideas as you like. For a luxurious look, use glitter and metallic cards to make up place cards, crackers, mats and coasters, then cut them out into graphic festive motifs, such as trees, crowns and stars. Festoon the table with paper chains and lanterns, or hang paper garlands along the back of chairs. Make individual party hats to wear while the cracker jokes are being told.

ABOVE LEFT This rustic Christmas table setting is decorated with crackers and cones made from brown packaging paper and pages torn from children's story books. These have been embellished with old laces and linen ribbons – a refreshing alternative to the brightly coloured plastic look that is so popular at this time of the year.

ABOVE RIGHT Pages from old annuals and story books have been torn out to make these ingenious paper cones, which can hold any small gift. Here, they have been used to hold marbles, but could also be used for chestnuts or mini mince pies.

RIGHT Make tiny gift bags suitable for holding sweets, or make larger versions for housing awkward-shaped gifts. Use a long rectangle of fibrous tissue paper, fold in half, then stitch up both free sides with a sewing machine, leaving the top open. Pop the gifts inside and tie closed with striped laces.

ABOVE These crackers have been made simply from brown paper and an illustrated gift tag. Use a shop-bought cracker kit, pile in paper hat, sweets and a joke, then wrap up and tie the ends neatly with a linen braid.

RIGHT Hang place cards on the back of chairs. Punch holes in the top corners of simple handwritten cards and thread through old stripy laces. If you can't find laces, use striped braid or ribbon instead.

To create symmetrical flowers, fold a piece of paper in four and cut a single petal shape (leaving the folded corner intact). Experiment with different colours and textures and transform your table setting from practical to sumptuous.

PROJECT 10: table runner

MATERIALS & EQUIPMENT
A1 ivory star-printed (or similar) paper
ivory textured paper
matt ivory textured paper
60 flower-shaped buttons
ivory thread • needle • scissors
ruler • glue

1. Take the A1 sheet of paper and tear it in half lengthways. Using the textured paper, cut twenty large flower shapes, measuring 12 cm (5 in) in diameter and twenty small flowers measuring 6 cm (2½ in) diameter. Cut twenty medium-sized flower shapes from the matt ivory paper measuring 9 cm (4 in) diameter.

2. Take one large flower and place the medium flower in the centre then place the smallest flower on top of that. Take a button and sew it to the centre of the twelve-petal flower. Repeat this with all the flower shapes until you have twenty flowers.

3. When all the flowers are complete, line them up along the long edges of the runner (ten on each side) and glue them into place.

4. Finally, take the rest of the buttons and place them in small groups along the runner. When you are happy with the arrangement of the buttons, sew them into position.

ABOVE This fresh, bright table setting is perfect for an alfresco summer lunch on the terrace.

LEFT Hot pink tissue paper has been stitched onto a pure white woven paper place mat to create a simple, yet effective, addition to the table.

OPPOSITE TOP RIGHT Pairs of chopsticks have been individually wrapped in blue paper pouches.

OPPOSITE RIGHT Paper napkins look sophisticated stacked high and held fast by a pebble paperweight decorated with Chinese silvered paper.

OPPOSITE FAR RIGHT Give your furniture a new lease of life by attaching colourful paper flowers to the back of tired wooden chairs. Cut out several petal-shaped layers of tissue paper, then thread a sequin through a thin length of florist's wire. Layer the tissue paper flowers on top of each other and secure with more wire, with the sequin in the middle. Twist the wire at the back of the flower to secure the layers.

decorative touches

Classic plain white china and good-quality glass- and silverware are the perfect starting point for any table setting. For an inexpensive and swift transformation, simply add paper accessories and your table will shout creativity and personality.

Everything from tablecloths, runners, mats and coasters to place cards, napkins and party favours can be made out of paper. While these accessories may not amount to very much individually, when laid out on your table in toning and contrasting colours they create a visual treat for your guests.

For example, take a fresh and bright Eastern theme for an alfresco summer lunch on the terrace. Contrast hot pink Chinese paper lanterns with the powder-blue Thai paper runners sitting on top of a white table-cloth. Fashion colourful paper flowers from tissue paper and attach them to the back of the chairs. Chopsticks individually wrapped in blue paper pouches and handwritten place cards complete the effect.

everything from tablecloths, runners and mats to place cards, napkins and favours can be made out of paper

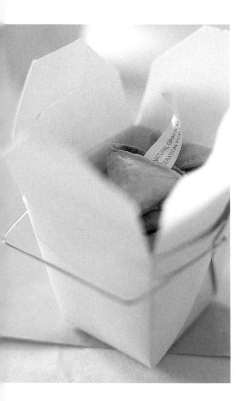

ABOVE LEFT Add to the Eastern theme with a dish full of after-dinner goodies. Wrap individual chocolates or sweets in paper parcels. Cut small squares of blue Japanese Asarkushi paper, place the confectionery in the centre of the square, then gather up the corners and tie up the bundle with white cotton.

LEFT AND ABOVE RIGHT Here, mini takeaway boxes are used as place-card holders. To make your own, clean a used takeout box, open it out and photocopy. Trace the template onto heavy white paper, cut out and fold together. Bend thin wire into a handle, pierce the side of the box and attach. Fill the boxes with fortune cookies for your guests to open up after dinner.

RIGHT These glasses have been decorated with zesty green tissue paper leaves, which have been attached to the stems with twisted wire. The tray is also made from paper. It has several layers of brown paper, created by Pierre Pozzi, bonded together with white glue and set to harden.

THIS PICTURE Elegant finishing touches make all the difference. Simple white and gold paper fans add to the Venetian carnival look.

INSET Metallic card masks are fun for a carnival-themed dinner party. Make up a template for the mask, use a craft knife to cut out the eye-holes and punch holes at each top corner. Embellish one corner with pearl beads and thread a ribbon through the punched holes. This way your guests can tie the masks on and keep their hands free for dinner.

Louise

Peonies are gorgeous, big, blousey flowers, but only in season for a short time at the height of summer. Tissue paper is a great medium for creating your own.

PROJECT 11: paper peonies

MATERIALS & EQUIPMENT
pink and dark green tissue paper
florists' wire • scissors • spoon • glue

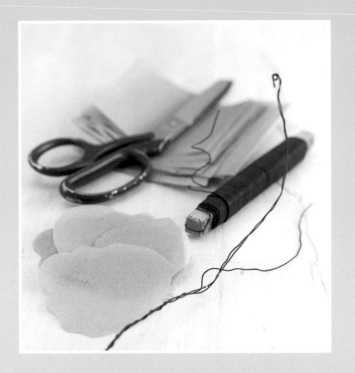

1. Cut a length of florists' wire, fold it in three and twist to make a thick stem. Make a knot at one end. Cut out petals of varying shapes and sizes from one sheet of pink tissue paper. One sheet of tissue paper will make enough petals for one flower.

2. Crumple the paper petals into tight balls and straighten them out to create a soft velvety texture. Use a spoon to mould and stretch the petals into curves.

3. To attach the petals to the wire, apply glue to the lower edge of the smallest petal and wrap around the knotted end of the wire. Build up the petals around the centre of the wire. Work the tissue petals into shape with your fingers as you go, overlapping each one and using larger petals as you progress.

4. When the flower is complete, turn your attention to the stem. Cut a long, thin strip of green tissue paper, approximately 1 cm (½ in) in width, glue along its length and wrap it around the wire. Cut a leaf shape from the green tissue paper and glue it onto the stem about a third of the way down.

special occasions

The cards and decorations used at occasions such as weddings, birthdays and special holidays are an essential part of the festivities. When coming up with new ideas to make the day more exceptional, paper is the perfect material. Invitations, greeting cards, flowers, bunting, confetti and party favours, though small, can all be made out of paper and make the day just that little bit more memorable.

ABOVE LEFT Intertwined initials of the bride and groom have been inscribed on a wedding gift tag.

ABOVE RIGHT A platter of tiny white card boxes has been customized with lace flowers.

OPPOSITE, CLOCKWISE FROM TOP LEFT Fill Washi packages with dried lavender for fragrant favours. Take a square of paper and place the lavender in the centre, fold in the top and bottom edges first, then either side. Hold the sides together and fold over at a slight angle, punch a hole through the folds and tie together with raffia twine; Guest books are adorned with beads and buttons; An elegant white guest book has a page mark made from a braid; Personalized thank-you notes are a pleasure to receive. Mount photos of the bride and groom or guests and, onto paper, write a thank you and roll into a scroll; A paper carton has been customized with a large fabric bow and a cord handle and filled with confetti. Make your own confetti by cutting lots of discs from layers of tissue paper.

wonderful weddings

Creating a dream wedding requires imagination. Pay attention to those inspiring little details that your guests will remember. From the wedding invitations, order of service and menus, to the place cards, table decorations and party favours, paper accessories can add a unique touch to your special day.

The main aim when putting together the details for a wedding is to achieve some kind of unifying theme. Often the dress or flowers will be the starting point of this creative process. Match up the paper to the texture or colours of the bride's gown. If the dress and flowers are variations of the traditional whites and creams, use natural shades of paper, allowing the textures to speak for themselves. A white watermarked invitation card, inlaid with soft white tissue and tied with a sheer white ribbon, looks elegant and sophisticated. This theme can be carried through to the table dressings, bunting – even the confetti.

Make coordinating invitations, place cards and favours for a wedding. The favour cone, which can be used to hold sugared almonds or mini chocolates, will delight your guests.

PROJECT 12: wedding paper goods

MATERIALS & EQUIPMENT
white cartridge paper
gift wrapping paper • glue
scissors • pencil • hole punch
brass paper fasteners
pink ribbons • sequin flowers

1. For the invitations and place cards, cut the cartridge paper to the size you require and fold in half. Cut a piece of wrapping paper, smaller than the card, and glue it onto the front of the card. Finally glue a length of ribbon down one side of the card and add a small sequin flower.

2. Use the template on p.104 and cut out the wedding favour cone from a piece of cartridge paper. Next, cut a curved triangle shape from the flocked gift wrap and glue it to the 'body' of the card (see above). Snip in the flaps from the outside curved edge up to the first dotted line.

3. Gently curve the cartridge paper into a cone shape and punch a hole at the top of each end (see above). Overlap the two holes and secure them together with the brass paper fasteners.

4. Begin to fold the flaps in towards the centre of the cone, trimming as you go, until they all meet in the middle. Put in your chosen favour, glue the last couple of flaps together and tie with a sheer pink ribbon.

christmas cheer

Christmas is the time of year when it's okay to go over the top with decorations and festive ornaments. Whether you like a restrained and elegant look or prefer to go mad with every colour under the sun, you can create great decorations with the humble piece of paper.

There are obviously Christmas cards to make, from the simplest stamped cards to those with elaborate pop-up and embossed details. Christmas gifts can be wrapped in themes to coordinate with the cards, or even with your homemade decorations. Embellish simple paper decorations with glitters, metallic paints and sequins to add that extra touch of sparkle. Hang ornaments with metallic thread and loop lengths of paper chains everywhere. Just imagine a tree twinkling under the weight of paper baubles, with a pile of gifts underneath, in complementing colours and the satisfaction that comes with knowing that you put the look together yourself.

Make it a family tradition to spend time together making paper decorations, stockings and paper chains, in the same way as you would decorate the tree or bake mince pies. You'll be amazed just how much fun it can be.

LEFT A simple tree decoration can double up as a gift. Take a square of paper and fill with flower seeds or dried lavender, then fold into a flat package, securing at the back with glue or tape. Cut out a metallic card star and add it to the front, punch a hole at the top and thread through a length of twine for hanging. These can be given out as little stocking fillers at Christmas.

BELOW A row of tea lights in small jam jars makes a cheap-and-cheerful Christmas window display.

Each jar has been topped with a metallic card crown. Cut a zigzag border along the top of a strip of card, bend into circles of the correct length, secured at the end, then simply pop them over the top of a jar.

RIGHT Festive wreaths needn't be made from spruce and berries, paper leaves can look striking. Photocopy old documents onto gold and white paper and cut these into laurel leaf shapes. Fashion a ring out of thin wire and arrange the paper leaves around it. Hang on walls inside your home.

RIGHT Hanging star garlands made from a variety of textured and detailed papers. Use a basic six-point star template to cut out a number of stars in different papers, then take a length of filament and glue the stars along its length. Hang from a window to get the full effect of the translucent paper.

BELOW LEFT AND RIGHT This oak-leaf wreath has been cut from newspaper. Finish off with tiny gold-sprayed rosehips.

FAR LEFT A plain papier mâché tree ornament has been decorated with tiny metallic star sequins. The card could be painted or covered in a metallic paper.

LEFT A flat star-shaped piece of card has been edged in gold paper and decorated with evenly spaced sequins in blues, gold and silver. Use this as a tree ornament, gift tag or greeting card.

BOTTOM FAR LEFT A tiny six-sided box, suitable for holding a small trinket, is tied with a floral braid and hung from a festive twig display.

BOTTOM LEFT This teardrop-shaped tree ornament has been embellished with metallic flower and star sequins. It looks stunning when hung on a twig display, emphasizing the natural colours and simple materials.

OPPOSITE These homely Christmas stockings, made out of brown packaging paper, make an interesting alternative to felts and shiny fabrics. Cut two identical stocking shapes from brown paper, separate them and decorate the front piece with paper discs, stars and sequins. Put the two pieces back together, matching up the edges. Sew them together, leaving the top opening free, using a large running stitch.

LEFT Adorn a small white gift box with heart-shaped confetti and a few leaf-shaped sequins, held together with a twist of jeweller's wire.

RIGHT There's something very special about a handmade Valentine's Day card. This one was made by photocopying a love poem and sticking it onto a blank card. Make the heart by folding a piece of flower-embedded paper in half, draw half a heart at the fold, cut out and unfold to reveal a perfectly symmetrical shape. Glue onto the front of the card.

BELOW These jewellery gift boxes have been given an extra romantic touch with elaborate red chiffon ribbon bows.

Valentine's Day

Valentine's Day derives from an ancient fertility celebration honouring Juno, a queen amongst the Roman gods. During this festival women would leave love letters in an urn for the menfolk to select at random. He would then pursue the woman whose missive he had chosen. It was like a love lottery. Christians, on the other hand, prefer to see it as a day for celebrating Saint Valentine, the patron saint of romantic causes. Either way, these days it's the one day of the year when it's okay to be openly romantic, showering loved ones with chocolates, flowers and cards.

Early Valentine's Day cards were made by hand, featuring paper lace, pin-pricked tissue and decoupage scraps. Carry on this tradition by making your own cards. Shop-bought cards are all very well, but there is nothing more romantic than realizing that your loved one has spent time and effort making something just for you. Or why not add a special touch to wrapped gifts and adorn special somethings with romantic imagery such as luscious lips, hearts and roses.

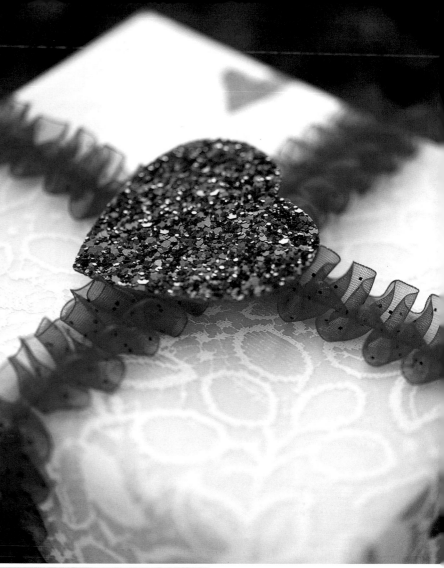

TOP LEFT Give a bunch of roses the Valentine's Day treatment by wrapping them in white tissue paper decorated with red hearts.

TOP RIGHT Here a red sheer braid, reminiscent of a garter belt, is topped with a red glittery heart.

LEFT Romance and candlelight go hand in hand, and this kind of lighting can set off any romantic evening. Cover glass votive holders with strips of paper doilies, which look like lace and diffuse the candlelight to a dim glow.

Easter

ABOVE Children's parties
are a great way to
practise papercrafting
techniques. Easter
parades, with the bonnets,
eggs and decorations,
can give you and the kids
a chance to explore papier
mâché.

RIGHT A necklace of
paper eggs has been
decorated with glitter,
paints and brightly
coloured tissue papers.
Blow eggs from their
shells and then cover
them in layers of white
glue and tissue.

Easter is a wonderful time of year. It is the start of a new season,
spring is in the air and chocolate takes pride of place everywhere.

The custom of giving eggs at Easter can be traced as far back as
the Egyptians. They had a custom of giving eggs at Spring Equinox,
which marked the beginning of the new season. The eggs
symbolized life and fertility. Christians later adapted this to the
story of the Resurrection. But to many of us Easter is a time
to enjoy chocolate eggs, children's parties and a good egg hunt.

It's a great time to pull out your crafting skills and make Easter
bonnets. Adorn paper hats with doilies, tissue and crêpe papers
and paper streamers in bright, pastel colours. Weave paper baskets
and fill them with papier mâché eggs, make nests out of shredded
paper and fill them with mini chocolate eggs. Choose papers
in sweet sugar almond colours – fresh blues, lavenders, daffodil
yellows and baby pinks to celebrate the end of winter.

TOP RIGHT Paint a selection of real eggs in bright pastel acrylic paints and then decorate in cut-out tissue paper shapes. The shapes can then be glued into place with white glue and sealed with a diluted white glue. The glue will be opaque when it is wet, but will dry clear.

CENTRE RIGHT These Easter bonnets have been made from a wide cone of coloured poster paper and bedecked with doilies, paper streamers and cut-out shapes.

BOTTOM RIGHT Tiny papier mâché eggs.

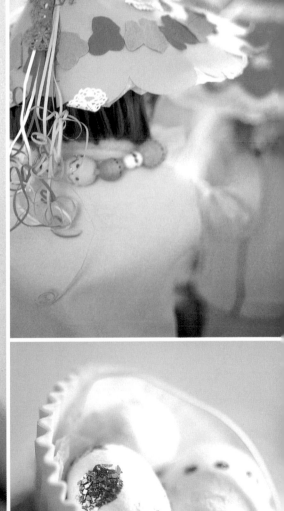

These decorative eggs look great arranged in a bowl as an Easter display. You can make use of all the spare scraps of paper in your craft box and be as creative as you like with the finishing touches.

PROJECT 14: Easter eggs

MATERIALS & EQUIPMENT
eggs • needle • wallpaper paste • paint
brush • pink and green tissue paper
patterned wrapping paper
scissors • PVA glue
sequins • jewels
selection of ribbons

1. Carefully make a hole the size of a pea in an egg, using a needle. Pour out the contents (make sure you break the membrane around the yolk with the needle). Wash the inside of the egg. Cover the eggshell with wallpaper paste or glue and attach a couple of layers of torn tissue paper. Let dry.

2. For the feathery eggs, cut out about forty small oval shapes from the patterned wrapping paper. Starting from the top, glue the oval shapes to the egg. Apply gule to the bottom of each oval, leaving the top free to overlap the layer above. Continue until the entire egg is covered.

3. For the stripy eggs, cut several small rectangular pieces of tissue paper and fold them into tiny strips. Glue them to the egg lengthways. Trim the excess paper and let dry.

4. For the finishing touches choose from the selection of sequins, jewels and ribbons and glue them to the egg to create a variety of effects. Remember to handle the egg delicately.

techniques

BINDING

The simplest way of binding the pages of a journal is to sew them together. First assemble the pages, then punch holes down one side. Sew the pages together with twine and tie the ends at the back of the journal.

COVERING

Open the book (or whatever you are covering), place it on a sheet of paper and draw around it. Cut the paper, leaving a 5 cm (2 in) border all the way around. Carefully fold in the border and secure with tape or glue. Snip into the paper at either edge of the spine, tuck the flap into the spine and secure with a dab of glue.

CUTTING

Large pieces of paper and card can be cut with a pair of scissors but a more precise cut can be achieved with a craft knife and self-healing cutting mat. When cutting straight lines use a metal ruler as a guide. Cut in a continuous motion. Ensure that the blade of the craft knife is very sharp, otherwise it will drag the paper and cause ragged edges. Always cut at a slight angle, away from yourself, to avoid any accidents.

DECOUPAGE

Decoupage is a papercrafting technique that first became popular in the Victorian times. It involves cutting out scraps and gluing them onto a surface, sealing and varnishing. This method is ideal for decorating anything from trays and boxes to screens.

Select your images and carefully cut them out using a craft knife. The images don't have to be printed, you could create your own patterns. Glue firmly onto the chosen surface (use a needle to push out any air bubbles) allow to dry and seal with diluted white glue.

EMBOSSING / IMPRESSING

Embossing can be done on most types of paper, as long as they are not too dense. If you are using a porous, matt textured paper, spray it lightly with water (to make the paper soft and malleable) before embossing.

If you are using an embossing tool, place the paper onto a soft surface – a pile of newspapers will do. Draw the chosen design (in reverse) on to the back of the paper and then inscribe over the drawing with the embossing tool, pushing heavily. When you turn the paper over the design will be standing out proud on the front.

FOLDING AND CREASING

Before folding a sheet of paper, first work out in which direction the grain goes (folding along the grain will ensure a sharp, neat fold). To do this, loosely bend the sheet, without creasing it, and notice how the paper springs back. Turn the sheet 90 degrees and repeat. You will notice a difference in the tension. When paper is folded along the grain it bends with little resistance.

Use a metal ruler to fold in a straight line and press along the fold with scissor handles for a sharp crease.

PAPIER MACHE

Making papier mâché is extremely simple and most of us will have the materials we need at home. Different combinations of paper and paste can be used, depending on the effect you want to create. Newspaper is most commonly used, but you can also use sugar, crêpe, brown and tissue paper – all of which will yield different colours and finishes. Wallpaper paste, a combination of flour and water paste and even diluted white glue all work.

There are several papier mâché techniques. The method used on p.59 is a basic layering technique, which involves soaking strips of paper in paste and layering them over a mould (the more layers you use, the thicker the finish).

Another way to make papier mâché is to create a pulp. Soak scraps of paper in warm water for at least 24 hours and then blend in a liquidizer. Put the pulp in a sieve and strain as much water out as possible. Transfer the pulp to a bowl, add white glue and mix until the mixture has a soft clay-like consistency. You could also add powder paint or food colouring to the mixture at this point. Mould the mixture into your chosen shape and let set.

SPRAY ADHESIVE

When using spray adhesive, ensure that you're working in a well ventilated, open space. Cover the back of the paper with a light, even layer of adhesive, spraying from side to side right up to the edges and then gently place into required position.

Spray adhesive doesn't dry immediately, which allows for some movement. It is ideal to use for precise and intricate work, the adhesive is clear and very thin, so it will not bubble or ooze out of the sides as glue can sometimes do.

USING TEMPLATES

Photocopy the template and enlarge or reduce accordingly. Transfer the image onto a thick paper or card and cut out. Place the temple on the back of your working paper and draw around it using a pencil. Place the paper face down onto the cutting mat and proceed to cut out using a sharp craft knife.

templates

snowflake

enlarge by 30%

stocking

enlarge by 30%

dove

enlarge by 30%

bauble

enlarge by 30%

angel

enlarge by 20%

castle

enlarge by 40%

wedding party favour

enlarge by 55%

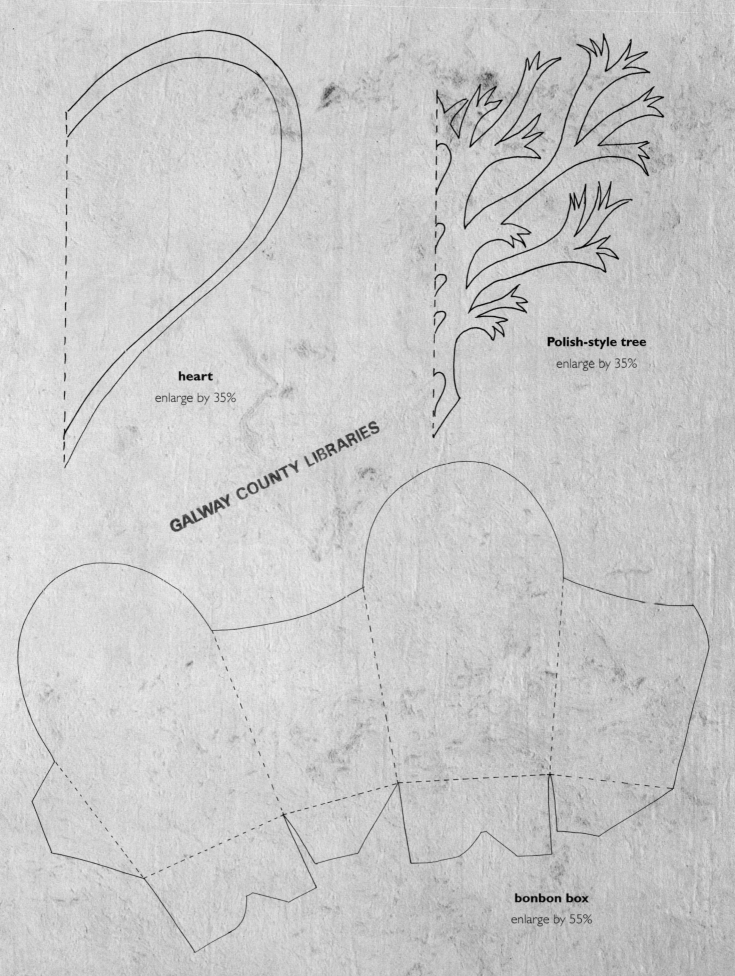

heart
enlarge by 35%

Polish-style tree
enlarge by 35%

bonbon box
enlarge by 55%

sources

ALEC TIRANTI
27 Warren Street
London W1P 5DG
t. 020 7636 8565
www.tiranti.co.uk
Embossing tools.

**ARJO WIGGINS
FINE PAPERS LTD**
Cateway House
PO BOX 88
Basingstoke
Hants RG21 4EE
t. 01256 723000
For a wide range of papers.

ATLANTIS EUROPEAN LTD
7–9 Plumbers Row
London E1 1EQ
t. 020 7377 8855
*Art supplies and a vast selection of
watercolour and cartirdge papers.*

BLACK MOUSE
www.blackmouse.co.uk
*DIY wedding stationery. Everything you
need from blank cards and envelopes
to trimmings.*

BLADE RUBBER STAMPS
12 Bury Place
London WC1A 2JL
t. 020 7831 4123
www.bladerubber.co.uk
Rubber stamps.

BUREAU
10 Great Newport Street
London WC2H 7JA
t. 020 7379 7898
*A wide selection of paper and card, art
materials, paper twine and ribbons.*

**CLARK CRAFT PRODUCTS
ONLINE**
www.clarkcrafts.co.uk
Paper, cards and general craft materials.

CONFETTI
80–81 Tottenham Court Road
London W1T 4TE
t. 020 7436 7177
www.confetti.co.uk
*Wedding invitations, cards, place
cards, pre-cut cards, envelopes and table
decorations.*

L CORNELISSEN & SON
105 Great Russell Street
London WC1B 3RY
t. 020 7636 1045
www.cornelissen.com
Gold leaf, decorative effects and papers.

COWLING AND WILCOX
26–28 Broadwick Street
London W1V 1FG
t. 020 7734 9557
www.cowlingandwilcox.com
*A wide selection of watercolour and
cartridge papers.*

CRAFT CREATIONS
Ingersoll House
Delamare Road
Chestnut
Herts EN8 9HD
t. 01992 781900
www.craftcreations.com
*Papers, cards, stamps, embossing tools,
everything you need to make cards.*

**THE DECORATIVE ARTS
COMPANY**
Basement, 5a Royal Crescent
London W11 4SL
t. 020 7371 4303
*Plain papier mâché items, including
decorations.*

DESIGNERS GUILD
267–71 Kings Road
London SW3 5EN
t. 020 7351 5775
www.designersguild.com
*A selection of brightly-coloured gift
wrapping papers, cards and accessories.*

DOVER BOOK SHOP
18 Earlham Street
London WC2H 9LG
t. 020 7836 2111
www.thedoverbooks.co.uk
*Copyright-free designs to use in
decoupage.*

THE ENGLISH STAMP COMPANY
Sunnydown
Worth Matravers
Dorset BH19 3JP
t. 01929 439117
*A wide range of stamps, stamping paint
and rollers.*

FALKINER FINE PAPERS
76 Southampton Row
London WC1B 4AR
t. 020 7831 1151
*Fine traditional papers, wax seals, book
binding and calligraphy equipment.*

FANTASY FAYRE
22 Camden Road
London NW1 9PD
www.fantasyfayre.com
Haberdashery and craft materials.

FRED ALDOUS
PO BOX 135
37 Lever Street
Manchester M60 1UX
t. 0161 236 2477
*Craft materials and equipment, including
embossing tools, decorative scissors, craft
knives, etc.*

HABITAT
196–199 Tottenham Court Road
London W1T 7PJ
t. 020 7631 3880
www.habitat.net
Funky gift wrap.

HEAL'S
196 Tottenham Court Road
London W1T 7LQ
t. 020 7636 1666
www.heals.co.uk
*A selection of gift wrapping paper and
stationery.*

HOBBYCRAFT
t. 0800 0272387
www.hobbycraft.co.uk
*Craft superstore with branches
nationwide.*

**HOLLOWAY ART AND
STATIONERS**
222 Holloway Road
London N7 8DA
t. 020 7607 4738
*Art and design materials as well as
a good range of watercolour papers.*

JOHN LEWIS
Oxford Street
London W1A 1EX
t. 020 7629 7711
www.johnlewis.com
*Good haberdashery and stationery
departments.*

KERNOWCRAFT
Bolingey
Perranporth
Cornwall TR6 0ZZ
t. 01872 573888
www.kernowcraft.com
*A selection of gemstones, crystals
and beads suitable for card-making
and embellishing.*

KLIENS
5 Noel Street
London W1F 8GD
t. 020 7437 6162
www.kliens.co.uk
A huge array of haberdashery, including diamanté buckles, textile trimmings and piping.

LAKELAND
www.lakelandlimited.co.uk
t. 015394 88100
branches nationwide
Card-making materials, including pre-cut cards, paper corners, borders, decorative scissors, and more.

LONDON GRAPHIC CENTRE
16–18 Shelton Street
London WC2H 9JL
t. 020 7210 0095
www.londongraphics.co.uk
Paper, card, graphic design equipment, paints, pens and craft tools.

MACCULLOCH AND WALLIS
25–26 Dering Street
London W1S 1AT
t. 020 7409 0725
www.macculloch-wallis.co.uk
Trimmings, including feathers and flowers.

THE MODEL SHOP
151 City Road
London EC1V 1JH
t. 020 7253 1996
www.modelshop.co.uk
All kinds of craft and model making supplies, including sculpels, glues and findings.

MUJI
www.muji.co.jp
A selection of plain brown paper products.

PAINTWORKS
99–101 Kingsland Road
London E2 8AG
t. 020 7729 7451
Art materials, pigments, paints, watercolour papers.

PANDURO HOBBY LTD
West Way House
Transport Avenue
Brentford
Middlesex TW8 9HF
t. 020 8847 6161
Art and craft materials.

THE PAPER SHED
www.papershed.com
A huge selection of papers, cards and paper products.

PAPERCHASE
213–215 Tottenham Court Road
London W1T 9PS
t. 020 7467 6200
www.paperchase.co.uk
A huge selection of papers from across the globe, cards, gift wrap, art materials and stationery.

PARTY PARTY
206 Kilburn High Road
London NW6 4JH
t. 020 7624 4295
Colourful paper decorations.

PARTY PARTY
11a Southampton Road
London NW5 4JS
t. 020 7267 9084
www.partypartyuk.com
Colourful paper tableware, streamers and decorations.

STANFORDS
12–14 Long Acre
London WC2E 9LP
t. 020 7836 1321
www.stanfords.co.uk
Maps, gift wrapping, luggage labels, stickers.

RYMAN
6–10 Great Portland Street
London W1N 5AA
t. 020 7637 0975
www.ryman.co.uk
All basic stationery needs, brown paper, sticking tape, scissors, etc.

SCRIBBLER
15 Shorts Gardens
London WC2 9AT
t. 020 7836 9688
www.scribbler.co.uk
Gift wrap and greeting cards.

SCRIVO
12 Holland Street
London W8 4LT
t. 020 7937 4000
Paper ribbons in all colours.

VV ROULEAUX
6 Marylebone Hight Street
London W1M 3PB
t. 020 7224 5179
www.vvrouleaux.com
Beautiful ribbons, braids, beads and haberdashery.

WOOLWORTHS
www.woolworths.co.uk
t. 0845 608 1101
branches nationwide
Basic stationery items, brown paper, tape, glues, stickers and glitter.

index

picture credits

Key: a=above, b=below, r=right, l=left, c=centre.

Endpapers ph Tom Leighton; page 1 ph Polly Wreford/styled by Claire Richardson; 2–3 ph Caroline Arber/designed and made by Jane Cassini and Ann Brownfield; 4al ph Jo Tyler/styled by Rose Hammick; 4bl ph Martin Brigdale/styled by Rebecca Duke; 4ar & 5 ph Polly Wreford/styled by Claire Richardson; 6b ph Caroline Arber/designed and made by Jane Cassini and Ann Brownfield; 6a, 7ac, 7ar & 7br all ph Polly Wreford/styled by Claire Richardson; 7al ph Carolyn Barber/styled by Lucy Berridge; 7bl ph Sandra Lane/styled by Mary Norden; 8–12 all ph Polly Wreford/styled by Claire Richardson; 13 inset ph Carolyn Barber/styled by Lucy Berridge; 13 main ph Polly Wreford/styled by Claire Richardson; 14–15 ph Sandra Lane/styled by Mary Norden; 16–17 ph Polly Wreford/styled by Claire Richardson; 18l ph Caroline Arber/designed and made by Jane Cassini and Ann Brownfield; 18r, 19al, bl & br ph Polly Wreford/styled by Claire Richardson; 19ar ph Sandra Lane/styled by Mary Norden; 20–21 ph Janine Hosegood/styled by Labeena Ishaque; 22al & 22b ph Polly Wreford/styled by Claire Richardson; 22–23a & 23ar Caroline Arber/designed and made by Jane Cassini and Ann Brownfield; 22–23b & 23br ph Polly Wreford/styled by Claire Richardson; 24–25 ph Janine Hosegood/styled by Labeena Ishaque; 26cl ph Polly Wreford/styled Margaret Castleton; 26al, ar, bl & 27–29 ph Polly Wreford/styled by Claire Richardson; 30–31 ph Sandra Lane/styled by Mary Norden; 32 ph Polly Wreford/styled by Claire Richardson; 33al, ac & bc ph Sandra Lane/styled by Mary Norden; 33ar & br ph Polly Wreford/styled by Claire Richardson; 33cl, c, cr & bl ph Carolyn Barber/styled by Lucy Berridge; 34–35 ph Janine Hosegood/styled by Labeena Ishaque; 36–37 all ph Polly Wreford/styled by Claire Richardson; 38a both ph Polly Wreford/styled by Claire Richardson; 38b ph Caroline Arber/designed and made by Jane Cassini and Ann Brownfield; 38–39a & 39br ph Polly Wreford/styled by Claire Richardson; 38–39b ph Carolyn Barber/styled by Lucy Berridge; 39ar ph Sandra Lane/styled by Mary Norden; 40–41 ph Janine Hosegood/styled by Labeena Ishaque; 42 all ph Carolyn Barber/styled by Lucy Berridge; 43al, ar & **background** ph Polly Wreford/styled by Claire Richardson; 43c & 44–45 ph Sandra Lane/styled by Mary Norden; 46–47 ph Polly Wreford/styled by Claire Richardson; 48al all ph Polly Wreford/styled by Claire Richardson; 48b ph Jo Tyler/styled by Rose Hammick; 49 ph Polly Wreford/styled by Claire Richardson; 50–51 ph Janine Hosegood/styled by Labeena Ishaque; 52al ph Sandra Lane/styled by Mary Norden; 52bl ph Caroline Arber/designed and made by Jane Cassini and Ann Brownfield; 52–53a & b & 53 ph Polly Wreford/styled by Claire Richardson; 54–55 ph Janine Hosegood/styled by Labeena Ishaque; 56–57 ph Polly Wreford/styled by Claire Richardson; 58–59 ph Janine Hosegood/styled by Labeena Ishaque; 60–61 ph Polly Wreford/styled by Claire Richardson; 62al & ar ph Polly Wreford/styled by Claire Richardson; 62b ph Caroline Arber/designed and made by Jane Cassini and Ann Brownfield; 63 both ph Polly Wreford/styled by Claire Richardson; 64 all ph Polly Wreford/styled by Mary Norden; 65al ph Polly Wreford/styled by Claire Richardson; 65ar, br & bl ph Caroline Arber/designed and made by Jane Cassini and Ann Brownfield; 66–67 ph Janine Hosegood/styled by Labeena Ishaque; 68al, ar & bl ph Polly Wreford/styled by Claire Richardson; 68br ph Caroline Arber/styled by Caroline Zoob; 69 all ph Polly Wreford/styled by Claire Richardson; 70–71 ph Janine Hosegood/styled by Labeena Ishaque; 72–75 ph Caroline Arber/designed and made by Jane Cassini and Ann Brownfield; 76–77 ph Janine Hosegood/styled by Labeena Ishaque; 78–80 all ph Polly Wreford/styled by Claire Richardson; 81 both ph Caroline Arber/designed and made by Jane Cassini and Ann Brownfield; 82–83 ph Janine Hosegood/styled by Labeena Ishaque; 84–85 ph Polly Wreford/styled by Mary Norden; 86l ph Caroline Arber/designed and made by Jane Cassini and Ann Brownfield; 86r, 87al & br ph Polly Wreford/styled by Mary Norden; 87ar, cr & bl ph Caroline Arber/designed and made by Jane Cassini and Ann Brownfield; 88–89 ph Janine Hosegood/styled by Labeena Ishaque; 90al ph Sandra Lane/styled by Mary Norden; 90br ph Jo Tyler/styled by Rose Hammick; 90–91a & 91ar ph Polly Wreford/styled by Claire Richardson; 90bl ph Sandra Lane/styled by Mary Norden; 90br ph Caroline Arber/designed and made by Jane Cassini and Ann Brownfield; 92–93 all ph Polly Wreford/styled by Claire Richardson; 94al & ar ph Polly Wreford/styled by Claire Richardson; 94b & 95ar ph Carolyn Barber/styled by Lucy Berridge; 95al & bl ph Polly Wreford/styled by Claire Richardson; 96–97 ph Janine Hosegood/styled by Labeena Ishaque; 98–99 all ph Polly Wreford/styled by Claire Richardson; 100–101 ph Janine Hosegood/styled by Labeena Ishaque; 102–109 ph Polly Wreford/styled by Claire Richardson; 110 ph Polly Wreford/styled by Mary Norden; 112 ph Polly Wreford/styled by Claire Richardson.

acknowledgments

Thanks very much to Janine Hosegood, a good friend and fantastic photographer, who worked so tirelessly to produce some beautiful photographs, despite being very pregnant at the time. Welcome to the world Maxwell! A big thank-you to the team at Ryland Peters & Small for their hard work and support, especially Miriam Hyslop and Catherine Griffin. Also to Anne-Marie Bulat, for giving me the opportunity to work on such great project. Love and best wishes to my family and friends. A special thank-you to Sam for doing pre-edit read-throughs and generally being a wonderful sister. Also to Gemma, thanks for lending me the boys' baby stuff, the gossip and drinks when I was suffering from cabin fever while writing during those dark winter days.